BYE BYE BIRDIE

Photos Courtesy of Hallmark Entertainment

ISBN 0-634-05778-2

HAL•LEONARD®
CORPORATION

7777 W. BLUEMOUND RD. P.O. BOX 13819 MILWAUKEE, WI 53213

In Australia Contact:
Hal Leonard Australia Pty. Ltd.
22 Taunton Drive P.O. Box 5130
Cheltenham East, 3192 Victoria, Australia
Email: ausadmin@halleonard.com

Visit Hal Leonard Online at
www.halleonard.com

SPARKLING NEW PRODUCTION OF "BYE BYE BIRDIE," STARRING JASON ALEXANDER, VANESSA WILLIAMS, CHYNNA PHILLIPS, TYNE DALY, GEORGE WENDT AND INTRODUCING MARC KUDISCH.

"Bye Bye Birdie," one of America's best-loved musicals, comes to television in a sparkling new production.

The special's stellar cast is headlined by Jason Alexander ("Seinfeld"), Vanessa Williams ("Kiss Of The Spider Woman"), Tyne Daly ("Cagney and Lacey"), George Wendt ("Cheers") and pop recording sensation Chynna Phillips. The title role of Conrad Birdie is played by Marc Kudisch ("Beauty and the Beast"). Broadway legend Gene Saks directs; choreography is by Ann Reinking ("All That Jazz").

In a delicious, tuneful parody of the Elvis pop phenomenon, composer Charles Strouse and lyricist Lee Adams invented Conrad Birdie, a wildly-popular, hip-gyrating '50's rock-n-roll star.

When Conrad is drafted into the U.S. Army, his manager, Albert Peterson (Jason Alexander) and Albert's devoted secretary, Rosie (Vanessa Williams), conjure up a publicity stunt: Conrad will make a final pre-induction appearance on "The Ed Sullivan Show."

The plan is to have the rock star bestow "One Last Kiss" on picture-of-innocence Kim MacAfee (Chynna Phillips in a live remote telecast from Sweet Apple, Ohio.)

The complications are, of course, both hilarious and tuneful. They're compounded by the presence of Kim's over-my-dead-body Dad (George Wendt) and Albert's domineering mother-from-Hell (Tyne Daly).

The great songs seem never to end in "Bye Bye Birdie": "How Lovely to be A Woman," "We Love You, Conrad," "Honestly Sincere," "One Last Kiss," "A Lot of Livin' to Do" and, of course, "Put on a Happy Face."

The executive producer of "Bye Bye Birdie" is Robert Halmi, Sr. ("Gypsy," "Scarlett"); J. Boyce Harman, Jr. ("Untamed Heart,") ("Royce") is the producer. Composer Strouse and Lyricist Adams have written two new songs for this production, which was filmed in Vancouver, British Columbia. It is from Hallmark Entertainment.

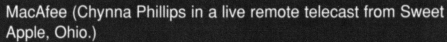

Photo by Ken Staniforth

BYE BYE BIRDIE

Lyric by LEE ADAMS
Music by CHARLES STROUSE

Bye Bye Birdie - 2 - 1

THE TELEPHONE HOUR

Lyric by LEE ADAMS
Music by CHARLES STROUSE

The Telephone Hour - 6 - 1

HOW LOVELY TO BE A WOMAN

Lyric by LEE ADAMS
Music by CHARLES STROUSE

How Lovely to Be a Woman - 4 - 1

15

16

PUT ON A HAPPY FACE

Lyric by LEE ADAMS
Music by CHARLES STROUSE

Put on a Happy Face - 2 - 1

A HEALTHY, NORMAL AMERICAN BOY
(We Love You, Conrad)

Lyric by LEE ADAMS
Music by CHARLES STROUSE

A Healthy, Normal American Boy - 12 - 1

22

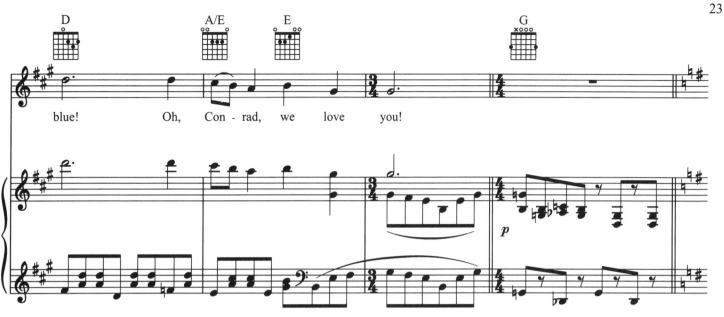

26

A Healthy, Normal American Boy - 12 - 7

28

A Healthy, Normal American Boy - 12 - 9

A Healthy, Normal American Boy - 12 - 10

ONE BOY (GIRL)

Lyric by LEE ADAMS
Music by CHARLES STROUSE

One Boy (Girl) - 2 - 2

HONESTLY SINCERE

Lyric by LEE ADAMS
Music by CHARLES STROUSE

Honestly Sincere - 6 - 1

36

Honestly Sincere - 6 - 4

E♭ F B♭ F♯7 G7
Oh, my ba - by, Oh yeah!
C F G7 C F G7 C C6
Group: "Yeah!"
Well, ya gon - na be sin - cere! Well, ya gon - na be sin - cere!
l.h.
C F G7 C F G7 C C6
"Yeah!"
Well, ya gon - na be sin - cere! Well, ya gon - na be sin - cere!
l.h.
C F G7 C F G7 C C6
"Yeah!"
Well, ya gon - na be sin - cere! Well, ya gon - na be sin - cere!
l.h.
C F G7 C
Oh, my ba - by, Oh, yeah! Oh,

LET'S SETTLE DOWN

Lyric by LEE ADAMS
Music by CHARLES STROUSE

Let's Settle Down - 3 - 1

42

HYMN FOR A SUNDAY EVENING
(Ed Sullivan)

Lyric by LEE ADAMS
Music by CHARLES STROUSE

Hymn for a Sunday Evening (Ed Sullivan) - 3 - 1

ONE LAST KISS

Lyric by LEE ADAMS
Music by CHARLES STROUSE

One Last Kiss - 2 - 1

A LOT OF LIVIN' TO DO

Lyric by LEE ADAMS
Music by CHARLES STROUSE

A Lot of Livin' to Do - 4 - 1

50

A Lot of Livin' to Do - 4 - 3

A Lot of Livin' to Do - 4 - 4

KIDS!

Lyric by LEE ADAMS
Music by CHARLES STROUSE

Kids! - 2 - 1

A MOTHER DOESN'T MATTER ANYMORE

Lyric by LEE ADAMS
Music by CHARLES STROUSE

(Spoken): So, it's come at last. At last it's come, the day I knew would come at last has come, at last. My sonny-boy doesn't need me any longer. Well, what are you waiting for? Get rid of me, put me out with the garbage; just throw me out with the used grapefruits and the empty cans from the tuna fish. And never mind putting a lid on it. Leave it open so a hundred thousand

A Mother Doesn't Matter Anymore - 8 - 1

A Mother Doesn't Matter Anymore - 8 - 2

A Mother Doesn't Matter Anymore - 8 - 4

58

60

A Mother Doesn't Matter Anymore - 8 - 7

61

A Mother Doesn't Matter Anymore - 8 - 8

A GIANT STEP

Lyric by LEE ADAMS
Music by CHARLES STROUSE

64

66 **Tempo**

A Giant Step - 5 - 5

ROSIE

Lyric by LEE ADAMS
Music by CHARLES STROUSE

Rosie - 5 - 1